Without a Mediator?

© 2025 Michael Richards
All rights reserved.

No part of this publication may be reproduced, stored in a retrieval system, or transmitted in any form or by any means—electronic, mechanical, photocopying, recording, or otherwise—without the prior written permission of the copyright owner, except in the case of brief quotations used in reviews or scholarly articles.

Unless otherwise noted, Scripture quotations are taken from the Holy Bible, King James Version (KJV)—Public Domain.

First Edition
ISBN: 978-1-7643453-0-9
Published by: Youth Sowing Truth

Cover illustration created using artificial intelligence.
Cover design by Michael Richards

Without a Mediator?

Recently, I've encountered significant opposition on the topic of Christ's mediatory work, particularly the belief that there will come a time when God's people must stand without a mediator.

What's the argument? First, perfection is unattainable, and therefore, we will always need Christ to mediate for us until He returns. Second, Jesus said he would never leave us. How can we stand without a mediator if He will never leave?

I am writing this brief pamphlet to bring clarity to this subject and to offer biblical evidence that brings hope—not fear—to those seeking truth.

What is a Mediator?

Before we delve into the subject, we need to

define the terms we are discussing. According to *Thayer's Greek Lexicon,* the Greek word translated as "mediator" in English means: one who intervenes between two, either in order to make or restore peace and friendship, or to form a compact, or for ratifying a covenant.

A mediator is, therefore, a go-between, someone who is present to facilitate peace and assists disputing parties in communicating, identifying issues, and exploring options for resolution.

Who is our Mediator?

There are only six references in the Bible that contain the English word 'mediator', and they are all found in the New Testament. The most commonly quoted one is 1 Timothy chapter 2 verse 5: "For there is one God, and one mediator between God and men, the man Christ Jesus." From this verse, we learn that there is one mediator that goes between us and God, and that person is Christ.

Without a Mediator

Christ is our mediator, the one who is "reconciling the world to himself" (2 Cor. 5:19). He is making peace between God and us.

Why do we need a Mediator?

Why does Christ need to make peace between God and us? The answer is simple: a separation has taken place. Once, we enjoyed a face-to-face relationship with God before Adam and Eve sinned. Since then, that communion has been broken. "But your <u>iniquities have separated</u> between you and your God, and your <u>sins have hid his face</u> from you, that he will not hear." (Isa. 59:2).

It is also clear, when we look at Revelation, what our actual condition is: "...knowest not that thou art wretched, and miserable, and poor, and blind, and naked." (Rev. 3:17). We are in this state because we have all "sinned, and come short of the glory of God." (Rom. 3:23). None of us are perfect; we are all sinful. If anyone wants

Without a Mediator

to argue that point, 1 John 1:10 says: "If we say that we have not sinned, we make him a liar, and his word is not in us."

This is precisely the reason a Mediator is necessary. Since "there is none that doeth good, no, not one." (Psa. 14:3). For anyone to have any hope in the judgment, we need a go-between to stand on our behalf because we cannot stand alone: "My little children, these things write I unto you, that ye sin not. And if any man sin, we have an advocate with the Father, Jesus Christ the righteous." (1 John 2:1).

Thankfully, Christ "ever liveth to make intercession for" us. (Heb. 7:25) He is that go-between, the mediator, the "Lamb slain from the foundation of the world" (Rev. 13:8), and it is only because of this fact that we are not consumed. "It is of the LORD'S mercies that we are not consumed, because his compassions fail not." (Lam. 3:22).

Without a Mediator

Will Christ's mediation end?

A logical question to ask at this point is: Will Christ's work as our Mediator ever end, and is there Biblical evidence to support it?

To understand this question, we need to recognise that the judgment is currently underway, which began in 1844 (Dan. 8:14).[1] Right now, Christ is standing as both judge and mediator. "For the Father judgeth no man, but hath committed all judgment unto the Son." (John 5:22); "I charge thee therefore before **God**, and the **Lord Jesus Christ**, who shall judge the quick and the dead at his appearing and his kingdom." (2 Tim. 4:1).

Every judgment must come to an end, and the Bible supports this concerning the investigative judgment. Daniel 12:1 says that Michael—

---

[1] This is the investigative judgment. We do not have enough space to give a detailed explanation of this in this pamphlet. For a more comprehensive understanding, refer to chapter 28 of The Great Controversy by Ellen G. White.

Without a Mediator

Christ—"stands up", symbolising judgment ending.

Throughout the last prophecy in Daniel, we find that whenever the word 'stand' is used, it signifies that a new power or kingdom will commence (Dan. 11:2-4, 16, 31).

We find that Christ is "set down at the right hand of the throne of God" (Heb. 12:2, see also chapter 8:1). We have already established that Christ is our mediator,[2] and from Daniel 7 we find that Christ has also entered the work of judgment.[3] One thing to note is that judgment begins only when the Father sits. We see from other bible stories that sitting symbolises the start of judgment—Pilate sat to judge Jesus; the council sat to judge Stephen; Festus sat to judge Paul.[4]

The opposite, then, is true: that when some-

---

[2] Heb. 7:25, 26; Rom. 8:34
[3] Daniel 7:9, 10, 13, 14
[4] John 19:13, Acts 6:15, Acts 25:17

Without a Mediator

one stands, it means that judgment is finished or has ceased. Therefore, when we examine the biblical imagery of Christ standing up, we must conclude that He has ceased interceding, and thus marks the close of probation—No more pleading; no more gospel message or call. The cleansing of the heavenly sanctuary is then complete.

An example of Christ standing is found in Acts chapter 7. Stephen, while being stoned, said, "I see the heavens opened, and the Son of man standing on the right hand of God" (v. 56). The stoning of Stephen marked the close of probation for the Jewish nation (Dan. 9:24-27), again showing that to stand is to cease whatever was taking place while seated—in this case, judgment.

It still occurs today in court; the judge remains seated while the case is being reviewed. Only when the judgment has been finalised does the judge stand.

Without a Mediator

Revelation supports this when it says, "He that is unjust, let him be unjust still: and he which is filthy, let him be filthy still: and he that is righteous, let him be righteous still: and he that is holy, let him be holy still" (22:11). This is a final statement; you cannot switch sides after it has been made, and it can only be made once judgment is finished.

At this point, you may ask, Why are we talking about judgment? I thought you were going to talk about Christ's mediation ending. The reason for examining a portion of the judgment is that, as mentioned before, Christ is both judge and mediator at the same time. You cannot have mediation after the judgment is finalised, so if we understand that the judgment will end, we know that Christ's mediation must also end at the same time. After all, Christ's mediation for us is directly linked to the judgment. If Christ does not mediate during the judgment, we have no hope.

Without a Mediator

A striking symbol of the end of Christ's mediation appears in Revelation 15:8, which says, "And <u>the temple was filled with smoke</u> from the glory of God, and from his power; and <u>no man was able to enter</u> into the temple, till the seven plagues of the seven angels were fulfilled."

Let's break down the key points of this verse. What does it mean when it says the temple was filled with smoke and that no man could enter it? To answer this, we must return to the Old Testament symbolism.

Each time the temple was filled with the glory of the Lord, no man could enter the temple, and thus no priest could minister in the sanctuary either.[5] The priest's purpose was to offer gifts and sacrifices for sin—to intercede on the sinner's behalf.[6] We find, then, that if the priest could not enter the sanctuary for ministration,

---

[5] Ex. 40:34, 35; 1 Kings 8:10, 11
[6] Hebrews 5:1; 7:25

there is no offering for sin—no intercession taking place.

Thus, we conclude that if no **man** can enter the sanctuary in heaven, then our mediator, "the **man** Christ Jesus", is no longer able to intercede on our behalf—no more ministering of the blood of Christ for sin; no more forgiveness; there is no longer an offer of mercy to the sinner; no one to stand between God and man.

It is at this point, when Christ stands and the temple is filled with smoke, that probation closes, and every person who is living on earth stands without a mediator until Christ returns, both righteous and unrighteous.

Why is this an issue for some?

It sounds scary to think that one day we will stand without a mediator, and it is often portrayed in a fearful light.

This topic was also frightening for me until I understood its true meaning. The way it is often

Without a Mediator

framed makes it sound like we will have to face the greatest time of trouble that has ever been, since there was a nation, and will ever be (Dan. 12:1), all without divine aid! That sounds terrifying, doesn't it? It's no wonder many find this thought unsettling.

Here's the good news: thankfully, we will not be alone. Many times, Jesus said that He would never leave us or forsake us. Here are a few verses showing this:

Hebrews 13:5 "...for he hath said, <u>I will never leave thee, nor forsake thee.</u>"

Matthew 28:20 "...and, lo, <u>I am with you alway, even unto the end of the world</u>. Amen."

Deuteronomy 31:6 "Be strong and of a good courage, fear not, nor be afraid of them: <u>for the LORD thy God, he it is that doth go with thee; he will not fail thee, nor forsake thee.</u>"

Without a Mediator

Romans 8:38-39 "For I am persuaded, that neither death, nor life, nor angels, nor principalities, nor powers, nor things present, nor things to come, Nor height, nor depth, nor any other creature, shall be able to separate us from the love of God, which is in Christ Jesus our Lord."

John 14:16 "And I will pray the Father, and he shall give you another Comforter, that he may <u>abide with you for ever</u>;"

Praise God! There is nothing to fear; although Christ's mediatorial role will come to an end, His presence, power, and love will remain with us forever.

What is perfection, and will we obtain it?

The word 'perfect' appears in 94 verses throughout the Bible. This is helpful, as many of

Without a Mediator

them provide insight into what perfection is and whether it's something we can attain.

Deuteronomy, talking about Christ, says, "He is the Rock, **his work is perfect**: <u>for all his ways are judgment: a God of truth and without iniquity, just and right is he</u>" (32:4). Here it is said that God's works are perfect. The verse then explains why His works are perfect: "for" (meaning because) His ways are judgment, and because He is truthful, without iniquity, just, and right.

Just from this verse alone, we can gain a clear understanding of what perfection is—living without iniquity, being just and right, and living truthfully. Simply put, it describes a life without sin.

Nearly everyone agrees that God is perfect, so let's consider what perfection looks like in humans.

There are a few people in the Bible who are described as being perfect. Probably the most well-known example is found in the book of Job.

Without a Mediator

Job is described as perfect, but what did that perfection look like?

In the very first verse of the book of Job, we are given a description of the man:

"There was a man in the land of Uz, whose name was Job; and that man was <u>perfect and upright, and one that feared God, and eschewed evil</u>."

Along with mentioning perfection, it also highlights other aspects of his life that help us understand what this perfection entails. Job feared God and eschewed evil. He was also upright.

The word 'eschewed,' in Hebrew, means to turn away from, withdraw from, or depart from or remove. Job actively turned away from evil, which means sin was not present in his life.

First Kings offers further insight into the subject. It states, "Let your heart therefore be perfect

Without a Mediator

with the LORD our God, to walk in his statutes, and to keep his commandments, as at this day" (8:61). From this verse, we understand that being perfect involves keeping God's commandments and walking in his statutes.

Jesus also said, "Be ye therefore perfect, even as your Father which is in heaven is perfect" (Matt. 5:48).

Biblical perfection is simply a life free from sin, characterised by avoiding evil, keeping the commandments, being truthful, and walking in the statutes of God.

The next question, then, is: Will and can we obtain this state here on earth before the coming of Christ?

The simple answer is yes, but not merely by keeping the law. True perfection involves more than simply adhering to strict laws. In fact, we cannot make ourselves perfect; there's nothing we can do in our strength to achieve it. (Phl. 2:13)

Without a Mediator

The following is a list of verses to support the idea:

"God is my strength and power: and <u>he maketh my way perfect.</u>" (2 Sam. 22:33)

"<u>I in them, and thou in me, that they may be made perfect in one;</u>..." (John 17:23)

"<u>That the man of God may be perfect</u>, thoroughly furnished unto all good works." (2 Tim. 3:17)

"<u>But let patience have her perfect work, that ye may be perfect and entire, wanting nothing.</u>" (James 1:4)

"And the very <u>God of peace sanctify you wholly</u>; and I pray God your whole spirit and soul and body <u>be preserved blameless unto the coming of our Lord Jesus Christ.</u>" (1 Thess. 5:23)

Without a Mediator

It is God in us that makes us perfect, not our own works.

The last verse is the key to answering the question proposed earlier. Reread it. What did it say? "<u>The very God of peace sanctify you wholly.</u>" This shows that God Himself is the one who sanctifies us. Sanctification is a daily process of surrendering the will to Christ, dying to self, and living for God in obedience to His law. It is the exercising of faith in His keeping power that enables us to live without sin, blameless, or perfect. Notice also that this state is to be reached before Christ comes, as the verse says, "<u>preserved blameless unto the coming of our Lord Jesus Christ.</u>"

With the above verses mentioned, it is clear that we are called to this experience on earth before His return. Just remember, we do not achieve this state of perfection by our own strength, but through faith in Christ's power working in us. After all, if we could do it on our own, why would we need Christ?

Why must Christ's mediation end?

To answer this, I would like to pose a simple yet essential question: Do you want to leave this world behind and return home? I hope you do. I certainly do.

The primary reason Christ's mediation must end is so that He can return, not as our High Priest, but as our King.

Right now, Jesus stands before the Father, mediating on our behalf. But once the judgment is complete and every case has been decided, His mediatorial work is finished. At that moment, He lays aside His priestly garments, puts on His kingly robes, and prepares to return. "And he was clothed with a vesture dipped in blood: and his name is called The Word of God. And he hath on his vesture and on his thigh a name written, KING OF KINGS, AND LORD OF LORDS." (Rev. 19:13, 16)

If His mediation never ends, then judgment is never concluded. And if judgment never ends, Christ will never return, and we will never go home.

That is why His mediation must come to an end. Not to abandon us, but to bring us home.

Why is all this good news?

From the outset, we have seen that a mediator is someone who serves as an intermediary between two parties to facilitate reconciliation. We have seen that Christ is our mediator, and He is so because of sin; without Him, we would be lost. We have observed that Christ's mediation will conclude at the same time as the end of the judgment. We have seen that although His mediation ends, He does not abandon us; He can be with us without being our mediator. We have also seen that perfection is something that we

Without a Mediator

can obtain and remain in a state of perfection until He returns, not through our own strength, but only as we put our faith in His keeping power. Finally, we saw that if Christ's mediation were never to end, we would never go home.

All this is excellent news because the end of Christ's mediation marks the beginning of something better: His return as King. It means the judgment has finished. It means every decision has been made. It means sin, suffering, and death are about to be dealt with forever.

"And God shall wipe away all tears from their eyes; and there shall be no more death, neither sorrow, nor crying, neither shall there be any more pain: for the former things are passed away." (Rev. 21:4)

"...Even so, come, Lord Jesus." (Rev. 22:20)

www.ingramcontent.com/pod-product-compliance
Lightning Source LLC
Chambersburg PA
CBHW061212070526
44583CB00025B/3226